The Present-Day Ministry of Jesus Christ

The
Present-Day Ministry of Jesus Christ

Kenneth E. Hagin

Second Edition
Fifteenth Printing 2006

ISBN 0-89276-014-1
ISBN-13: 978-0-89276-014-5

In the U.S. write:
Kenneth Hagin Ministries
P.O. Box 50126
Tulsa, OK 74150-0126
1-888-28-FAITH
www.rhema.org

In Canada write:
Kenneth Hagin Ministries
P.O. Box 335, Station D
Etobicoke (Toronto), Ontario
Canada, M9A 4X3
www.rhemacanada.org

Contents

Chapter 1
Jesus Christ, Our High Priest

But Christ being come an high priest of good things to come, by a greater and more perfect tabernacle, not made with hands, that is to say, not of this building;

Neither by the blood of goats and calves, but by his own blood he entered in once into the holy place, having obtained eternal redemption for us.

— Hebrews 9:11,12

The high priestly ministry of Christ at the right hand of the Father is one of the rarest features of the revelation given to the Apostle Paul.

In the epistles, Paul not only tells us what Christ did for us in His substitutionary work on the cross; he also tells us what the Holy Spirit does in our individual lives.

Many theologians and scholars question the authorship of the Book of Hebrews. Some do not think Paul is the author. I believe, however, that it is quite conclusive that this book is part of the Pauline revelation, because Hebrews fits into it like part of a jigsaw puzzle, and the language is that of Paul.

The Book of Hebrews is a revelation of what Jesus did from the time He was made sin on the cross, until He sat down on the right hand of Majesty on High. Christ's entire redemptive work is shown in this wonderful unveiling in Hebrews. There are references to this work elsewhere in the New Testament, but this revelation is found primarily in Hebrews.

There are four phases to this revelation that God gave Paul:

1) What God, through Christ, did for us in His great substitution;

2) What the Holy Spirit, through the Word, does in us in the New Birth and the infilling of the Holy Spirit;

3) What Jesus is doing for us now in His present-day ministry at the right hand of God;

4) What God's Word and His love do through us in ministering.

Through the years, we believers have spent a great deal of time studying what Christ had done for us. Most sermons are along that line. However, very little time has been spent studying what He does *in* us. And even less time has been spent studying what He is doing for us *now* in His great high priestly office at the right hand of the Father. Yet His entire ministry for us would not have been complete if He were not carrying on a ministry now in our behalf at the right hand of God.

Jesus' first ministry after His *resurrection* is mentioned in John 20:

JOHN 20:11,15-17
11 But Mary stood without at the sepulchre weeping: and as she wept, she stooped down, and looked into the sepulchre . . . .
15 Jesus said unto her, Woman, why weepest thou? whom seeketh thou? She, supposing him to be the gardener, saith unto him, Sir, if thou have borne him hence, tell me where thou hast laid him, and I will take him away.
16 Jesus saith unto her, Mary. She turned herself,

**and saith unto him, Rab-
boni; which is to say, Master.
17 Jesus saith unto her,
Touch me not; for I am not
yet ascended to my Father:
but go to my brethren, and
say unto them, I ascend
unto my Father, and your
Father; and to my God, and
your God.**

Christ is not talking in this
passage about His *ascension* and
being seated at the right hand of
the Father, because just a short
time later He appeared again; this
time to His disciples. (His actual
ascension didn't happen for many
days afterwards.) The disciples
thought He was a ghost, but He
said, *". . . handle me . . . for a spirit
hath not flesh and bones . . ."* (Luke
24:39).

Why did Jesus say to Mary,
"Touch Me not"; yet a short time
later He instructed His disciples
to touch Him? Because when
Mary saw Him, He was on His

way to enter into the heavenly Holy of Holies to present His blood as an eternal offering or sacrifice for our sins.

Jesus died as a Lamb, but He arose as the Lord High Priest! And the Word tells us that He is a merciful and faithful High Priest; not just in things pertaining to men, but also in things pertaining to God:

> **HEBREWS 2:14-17**
> **14 Forasmuch then as the children are partakers of flesh and blood, he also himself likewise took part of the same; that through death he might destroy him that had the power of death, that is, the devil;**
> **15 And deliver them who through fear of death were all their lifetime subject to bondage.**
> **16 For verily he took not on him the nature of angels; but he took on him the seed of Abraham.**

17 Wherefore in all things it behoved him to be made like unto his brethren, that he might be a merciful and faithful high priest in things pertaining to God, to make reconciliation for the sins of the people.

The claims of Justice had to be satisfied in things pertaining to God. It was necessary that Christ as a High Priest make propitiation for the sins of the people. He had to carry His blood into the heavenly Holy of Holies and seal the document of our redemption with it.

HEBREWS 9:11,12
11 But Christ being come as an high priest of good things to come, by a greater and more perfect tabernacle, not made with hands, that is to say, not of this building;
12 Neither by the blood of goats and calves, but by his own blood he entered in once into the holy place,

**having obtained eternal
redemption for us.**

Under the Old Covenant,
which Paul is referring to here,
the High Priest entered the Holy
of Holies once a year and offered
the blood of innocent animals
slain as a sacrifice for the sins of
the people. Thus, the people's sins
would be *covered* for another year.

*But Christ entered in once for
all*. This is one ministry He never
has to repeat: He does not enter
the Holy of Holies year after year
as the high priest of old did. He
entered in once and for all to
obtain an *eternal redemption* for
us. His blood is the guaranty, so
to speak, of our redemption.

That is what He was on the
way to do when Mary saw Him
and He told her, "Don't touch me."
He already had taken care of our
redemption when the disciples

saw Him a little later, because He said, "Now you can touch Me."

Afterwards, when Christ ascended to heaven and sat down at the right hand of the Father, He began another ministry, an ongoing high priestly ministry as our Advocate, Mediator, Intercessor, and Shepherd.

The word translated "atonement" in Romans 5:11 is actually "redemption." "Atonement" is an Old Testament word which simply means to *cover* the sins of Israel while the sins were borne away by the scapegoat.

The nature in man that had caused him to sin remained to be dealt with — that nature in man that made him lie, steal, and break the law. Under the New Covenant, Jesus dealt with that sin-nature. *He took that nature away by the sacrifice of Himself.*

HEBREWS 9:24-26
24 For Christ is not entered into the holy places made with hands, which are the figures of the true; but into heaven itself, now to appear in the presence of God for us:
25 Nor yet that he should offer himself often, as the high priest entereth into the holy place every year with blood of others;
26 For then must he often have suffered since the foundation of the world: but now once in the end of the world hath he appeared to put away sin by the sacrifice of himself.

Notice the scripture doesn't say "sins." Sins are deeds or acts that are wrong. It says, "sin," referring to man's sin-nature — the thing that caused him to do what he did.

HEBREWS 9:28
28 So Christ was once offered to bear the sins of

**many; and unto them that
look for him shall he appear
the second time without sin
unto salvation.**

Christ not only bore our
sins — our deeds and acts of
wrongdoing — He also bore our
sin — man's sin-nature.

After all, it would not do me
any good for Christ to bear just
my sins — I still would have that
old sin-nature in me, and I could
not help but do wrong. I still
would be the same kind of creature I always had been. But
when He put away sin by the sacrifice of Himself, Jesus did something about that sin-nature that
caused me to sin. And He did it
once and for all.

When I accepted Jesus as my
Savior and confessed Him as my
Lord, the Holy Spirit did something in me. This is also part of
the Pauline revelation not found

anywhere else in the New Testament.

For example, Second Corinthians 5:17 says, *"Therefore if any man be in Christ, he is a new creature: old things are passed away* [Do you know what this old thing is that passed away? It is the old sin-nature]; *behold all things are become new."* You have a new nature inside! At the very moment you were born again, that inward nature was changed!

I found that true in my own life. I had never heard it preached, but I discovered immediately after being born again that the things I had been so concerned about were gone. My nature was changed. The things I once loved I no longer loved. The things I once hated I now loved. The "want-to" or desire to do wrong was gone. (That doesn't mean that I haven't failed since then.)

Under this Dispensation of the Holy Spirit, we have a better covenant! Through the New Birth that we experience, Christ took away our old sin-nature and gave us the life and nature of God. The "want-to" toward sin is gone.

The destruction of our sin-nature required, however, that God's beloved Son become sin for us:

2 CORINTHIANS 5:21
21 For he hath made him to be sin for us, who knew no sin; that we might be made the righteousness of God in him.

No wonder Jesus cried out on the Cross when He was made to be sin, *"My God, my God, why hast thou forsaken me?"* (Matt. 27:46).

God had forsaken Him because He was taking our place. He became what we were. He took our sin that we might become righteous. He took our spiritual death that we might have eternal life. He took our ostracism, our outlawed nature, that we might become sons of God.

How marvelous is the unmeasured grace of God as unveiled in the sacrifice of Jesus! Jesus carried His own blood into the heavenly Holy of Holies, thus cancelling the need for the High Priest to make an annual atonement. Instead, Jesus gave us *eternal redemption*!

Jesus was made sin. He was under condemnation because we were under condemnation. For three days and nights He was locked up in the prison house of death because that is where we should have gone. He became our Substitute and took our place. He met the demands of Justice and liberated us! Until then, no one could be born again. The Old

Testament believers were not born again.

They were saved as far as God's plan of salvation then was concerned — their sins were forgiven — but they were not born again.

If you sin after you are born again, you can confess your sins and God will forgive you (1 John 1:9), but you aren't born again a second time. No one is ever born again twice. If you were born again every time your sins were forgiven, some people would be born again a million times. You can't be made a new creature more than once.

In the Old Testament we read that So-and-so begat So-and-so. It was necessary that the Jews keep their genealogy. Under the New Covenant, however, we can write our genealogy in four words: *"Ye are of God . . ."* (1 John 4:4). We are born of God!

Chapter 2
Jesus Christ, Our Advocate

If we confess our sins, he is faithful and just to forgive us our sins, and to cleanse us from all unrighteousness.

If we say that we have not sinned, we make him a liar, and his word is not in us . . . .

My little children, these things write I unto you, that ye sin not. And if any man sin, we have an advocate with the Father, Jesus Christ the righteous:

And he is the propitiation for our sins: and not for ours only, but also for the sins of the whole world.
— 1 John 1:9,10; 2:1,2

The word "advocate" means *lawyer*, or *one who pleads our cause or case*. When the believer is tempted and Satan gains mastery over him, the believer can claim the promise of First John 1:9, *"If we confess our sins, he is faithful and just to forgive us our sins, and to cleanse us from all unrighteousness."*

The Apostle John went on to say, *"My little children . . ."* (1 John 2:1). Man put the artificial divisions between these chapters; John did not write in chapter and verse like this. Therefore, reading the four verses of our text *in sequence*, we can see that John was not writing to sinners; he was writing to Christians.

First John 1:9 often is quoted to sinners, telling them to confess their sins. God didn't tell them to. It would be impossible for a sinner to confess every wrong he had ever done, because his whole life is wrong! No, this verse was written to Christians.

John writes, *"My little children* [because they were saved under his ministry and were his spiritual children], *these things write I unto you, that ye sin not. And if any man sin, we have an advocate with the Father, Jesus Christ the righteous."*

This brings us to a very sensitive subject in the Church world. Instead of staying with what the Bible says, some groups divide into theological circles or cliques that accept certain concepts whether they are scriptural or not.

It seems that the Church world as a whole is divided into two groups: Calvinists and Arminians.

In the 16th century, John Calvin and Jacobus Arminius attended the same institute of learning, but each came out with a different idea. One result is what we call "old school Calvinism," which embraced predestination, or "what is to be will be."

During the time of the famed evangelist Charles Finney, the ministers of that day had been taught Calvinism in the Yale School of Divinity. They believed that if you were predestined to be saved, you would be saved. If you were not predestined to be saved, there was nothing you could do about it. You could join the church and take advantage of its benefits, but God would save you only if it were His will.

Finney was a lawyer. After he finished his education, he began to practice law with a former judge. The judge suggested that Finney join a church because it would help him with business and social contacts. Finney did so. In one of the young people's services, he asked them to pray for him, because he realized he was unsaved and did not know God.

The group was astonished at his request, telling him that if he were predestined to be saved he would be; otherwise, he would be lost.

Finney began to read his Bible. The more he read, the more he was convinced that he could be saved — and everyone else could, too, if they wanted to be. Alone, he sought God and was born again.

He soon became a minister and preached that when God said in His Word "Repent," He meant you could do it. (The Calvinists preached that you could not repent unless God gave you a repenting heart; that you were totally incapable of doing anything yourself.)

Finney preached that if God asked you to do something you

couldn't do, then He would be an unjust God — but God is not unjust — and when He said, "Believe," He meant you can believe. (The Calvinists, however, felt you could not believe unless God gave you a believing heart.)

Today, there are not too many old school Calvinists — their doctrines have been watered down — but now there are "new school Calvinists." "New school Calvinism" is basically the doctrine of eternal security, or "once saved always saved."

I believe in eternal security *as long as you stay in Christ*. He is able to keep you secure. But just because you are a son of God does not mean you are not a free moral agent. You still have a will of your own, and you can choose to stay in Christ or forsake Christ altogether.

The Arminian side is not correct, either. They think that when you commit the smallest sin you are immediately lost and need to be saved all over again.

Arminians have the idea that God is like a fellow with a fly-swatter — just waiting for a fly to light so He can swat it. They think God is waiting for His children to make just one mistake — and when they do, He is going to swat them!

One man said he believed that if he were to speak harshly to his wife, he would be lost and bound for hell. He believed he would have to get saved all over again. If that were true, there are some people who have been saved 2,000 or 3,000 times a day!

Then there are those who believe that God expects us to live above sin. They believe in going on to perfection. I do too, but I haven't arrived there yet. If we already were perfect, we would not have anything to go on to.

Paul said, *"Brethren, I count not myself to have apprehended: but this one thing I do, forgetting those things which are behind, and reaching forth unto those things which are before"* (Phil. 3:13).

When you teach about this subject, someone always believes you are giving people a license to sin. I always say, however, that people do enough sinning without a license!

It is quite obvious that God does not want us to sin: *". . . these things write I unto you, that ye SIN NOT"* (1 John 2:1). It is quite obvious that if we walked completely in the Word and in love, we wouldn't sin. But it is also obvious that none of us have achieved this yet.

Considering the other side of the question, there are those whose Christian conversion I doubt; I doubt that they were ever Christians. Why? Because they have been taught a degree of Calvinism, they live any way they like and do anything they like — cheat, lie, and steal.

Some have said to me, "It doesn't make any difference what I do. Christ is my Advocate." One man said, "I don't know but what I might steal a mule next week. I am not planning to do it, but if I do, Jesus already has forgiven me for it." I doubt seriously if a fellow like that was ever saved.

This scripture in John never was intended to encourage people to sin. John is simply telling us about God's provision *for* sin. The Spirit of God will help us overcome sin; not encourage us to practice it! After all, John said, *"These things write I unto you, that you sin not."*

In the first place, if a man is born again — if he knows God — he doesn't want to do wrong. But often the devil tempts him through his flesh and overcomes him because he is not strong spiritually.

Paul said, *"Brethren, if a man be overtaken in a fault, ye which are spiritual, restore such an one in the spirit of meekness; considering thyself, lest thou also be tempted"* (Gal. 6:1).

If it were just a fault Paul was talking about, we all would need restoring, and there wouldn't be any spiritual people left to do the restoring. We all have faults. The Greek actually says, "If any man among you be overtaken in an offence, or sin, you which are spiritual, restore such a one in the spirit of meekness."

God wants His people to be restored to full fellowship with Him. It is a different matter, however, when people do not want to be restored. If they want to be restored, it is our obligation to restore them in a spirit of meekness, not arrogance. Why? " . . . *considering thyself, lest thou also be tempted,*" Paul says.

When it comes to healing, James 5:14 and 15 says, *"Is any sick among you? let him call for the elders of the church; and let them pray over him, anointing him with oil in the name of the Lord: And the prayer of faith shall save the sick, and the Lord shall raise him up; and if he have committed sins, they shall be forgiven him."* We see here the possibility of sin.

If a man were to speak sharply to his wife, he is not lost because of it. He *is,* however, out of fellowship with her! He needs to get back in fellowship with her by apologizing and asking her forgiveness.

" . . . *If any man sin, we have an advocate with the Father, Jesus Christ the righteous"* (1 John 2:1).

If we sin, we lose the sense of righteousness and cannot enter God's Presence. Righteousness means right standing with God. Righteousness means the ability to stand in the Presence of God without any inferiority complex, without a consciousness of sin.

If you have sinned or failed, you cannot stand in the Presence of God without a consciousness of sin. But there is One who can go in on your behalf — Jesus Christ, the Righteous. He is the propitiation — the substitute — for our sins; and not for our sins only, but for the sins of the whole world.

As our Advocate, Jesus restores to us our lost sense of righteousness, for He said, "*If we confess our sins, he is faithful and just to forgive us our sins . . .*" (1 John 1:9). But He does more than just forgive us of our sins; He cleanses us from all unrighteousness. He cleanses us from that sin-consciousness or spiritual inferiority complex that would keep us from coming to God.

There are those who live under a cloud of fear. They say things like, "I am so afraid of displeasing the Lord. If Jesus comes, I might not make it. I don't know if I am ready or not." And they are robbed of their joy in Christ. They are afraid that God is mad at them and will not have anything to do with them.

We do not have to live under such a cloud of fear and gloominess. We can know that if we have failed — if we are Christians — our hearts will be grieved about it. If you can keep on sinning and failing, however, and are *not* grieved about it, you had better check up on your Christian experience. If you have been born again and have the life and nature of God in you, you don't want to do wrong.

Many times new Christians miss God's will and sin in ways they are not even aware of, but they are walking in the light they do have. *"But if we walk in the light, as he is in the light, we have fellowship one with another, and the blood of Jesus Christ his Son cleanseth us from all sin"* (1 John 1:7).

As I look back now, after more than sixty years of being a Christian, I can see that I missed God many times when I didn't even know it. At the time, I walked in what light I had, and the blood of Jesus Christ cleansed me from things I didn't know about.

I can remember the first time I was conscious of the fact I had done wrong after I became a Christian. It nearly broke my heart.

If a believer is tempted and Satan gains mastery over him on something, when the believer cries out for mercy, he can hear Christ whisper, *"If we confess our sins, he is faithful and just to forgive us our sins, and to cleanse us from all unrighteousness"* (1 John 1:9).

And then we also can hear Him say in this marvelous scripture from Hebrews 4:16, *"Let us therefore come boldly unto the throne of grace . . ."* Why? *". . . That we may obtain mercy . . . ."* It is *mercy* we need when we have sinned. As long as we are doing right, we can get by on *justice*.

In Hebrews 4:14 we read, *"Seeing then that we have a great high priest . . . ."* We have a High Priest who also stands in this office of Advocate that we may *" . . . come boldly unto the throne of grace, that we may obtain mercy, and find grace to help in time of need."*

Grace is unmerited favor. When you fail is the time you need grace; that's when you need mercy.

Once while driving through a small town, a minister friend of mine drove through a red light. Before he knew it, there was a flashing red light behind him and the sound of a shrill siren. A policeman pulled him over and gave him a ticket for running a red light and for going 45 in a 30 mph zone.

When the minister had to appear in court, his case was stated and the judge asked if he had anything to say.

He answered, "Yes, I do." He explained that he was on his way to preach; that he ministered in small country churches. Then he said, "Judge, I don't have a dime. I'll just have to go to jail or work it out on the county farm. I'm not going to ask for justice. I would be in trouble if I got justice, because

I'm guilty. So I am asking instead for mercy."

He continued, "I'm like the woman in the Bible who was taken in the act of adultery. Her accusers brought her to Jesus, and He said, ' . . . *He that is without sin among you, let him first cast a stone at her*' [John 8:7]. He stooped down to write something in the sand, and when He looked up, everyone was gone.

"*'When Jesus had lifted up himself, and saw none but the woman, he said unto her, Woman, where are those thine accusers? hath no man condemned thee? She said, No man, Lord. And Jesus said unto her, Neither do I condemn thee: go, and sin no more'*" (John 8:10,11).

The preacher added, "I am asking for mercy, and I'll go and sin no more."

The judge asked, "Is that story in the Bible?"

"Yes," the preacher answered.

The judge said, "I wish you would show it to me." The preacher had his New Testament with him, so he turned to that passage and showed it to the judge.

The judge said, "I teach a Sunday school class in the Methodist church, but I didn't know that was in there. I'm going to teach on that. Case dismissed!"

The judge showed mercy. If the preacher hadn't been speeding and hadn't run that light, he would have gotten by on justice; he wouldn't have needed mercy. But he broke the law and therefore needed mercy.

Mercy and grace are always available to us when we break God's law. All we need to do is call on Christ our Advocate.

Chapter 3
Jesus Christ, Our Intercessor

Seeing then that we have a great high priest, that is passed into the heavens, Jesus the Son of God, let us hold fast our profession.

For we have not an high priest which cannot be touched with the feeling of our infirmities; but was in all points tempted like as we are, yet without sin.

Let us therefore come boldly unto the throne of grace, that we may obtain mercy, and find grace to help in time of need.

— Hebrews 4:14-16

This portion of Scripture carries us a step further in our study of Christ's high priestly ministry. Jesus is the High Priest of the New Covenant. The high priest of the Old Covenant had certain duties to perform. We discussed in chapter one how he entered into the Holy of Holies once a year with the blood of animals to receive an atonement for the sins of the people.

Just as the high priest under the Old Covenant had more duties to perform than that annual function, so it is with Jesus. Although He entered into the heavenly Holy of Holies once and for all with His blood to obtain redemption for us, He still stands today in the office of High Priest.

Another office Jesus fills today is that of Mediator. He is the mediatorial High Priest between God and man. No man can reach the Father except through Christ.

Jesus said, ". . . *I am the way, the truth, and the life . . .* " (John 14:6). One translation reads, "I am the way, the reality, and the life." Christ is the only way to God.

Peter said in Acts 4:12, *"Neither is there salvation in any other: for there is none other name under heaven given among men, whereby we must be saved."*

Another translation reads, "And in none other is there salvation, for neither is there any other name under heaven that is given among men, whereby we must be saved." Only through Jesus can we enter the Father's Presence without condemnation.

The Early Church was often called "the Way." Let us look at a few scriptures found in the Acts of the Apostles:

ACTS 9:2

2 And desired of him letters to Damascus to the synagogues, that if he found any of THIS WAY, whether they were men or women, he might bring them bound unto Jerusalem.

This scripture refers to Saul of Tarsus, who had letters in his possession from the authorities, giving him the power to arrest any person he found who were members of "the Way."

ACTS 19:9

9 But when divers were hardened, and believed not, but spake evil of THAT WAY before the multitude, he departed from them, and separated the disciples, disputing daily in the school of one Tyrannus.

Another translation reads, "When some were hardened and

were disobedient, speaking evil of the way."

ACTS 19:23
23 And the same time there arose no small stir about THAT WAY.

ACTS 24:14
14 But this I confess unto thee, that after THE WAY which they call heresy, so worship I the God of my fathers, believing all things which are written in the law and in the prophets.

ACTS 24:22
22 And when Felix heard these things, having more perfect knowledge of THAT WAY, he deferred them, and said, When Lysias the chief captain shall come down, I will know the uttermost of your matter.

ACTS 16:17
17 The same (A damsel possessed with a spirit of divination.) **followed Paul and us,**

**and cried, saying, These men
are the servants of the most
high God, which shew unto
us THE WAY of salvation.**

Even the devil called it "the
way," didn't he? This last verse is
taken from a passage that tells
the story of a young woman possessed with the spirit of divination, or fortune-telling, who
followed Paul and Silas through
the streets of Philippi, saying,
"*. . . These men are the servants of
the most high God, which shew
unto us the way. . . .*"

So not only is Christ the Lord
High Priest; He is also the Mediator — the only way that the sinner can get to God.

The moment a person accepts
Christ, Jesus becomes his or her
high priestly Intercessor! The
Bible tells us that He ever lives to
make intercession for believers:

HEBREWS 7:25

25 Wherefore he is able also to save them to the uttermost that come unto God by him, seeing **HE EVER LIVETH TO MAKE INTERCESSION FOR THEM.**

ISAIAH 53:12

12 ... he hath poured out his soul unto death: and he was numbered with the transgressors; and he bare the sin of many, and made intercession for the transgressors.

ROMANS 8:34

34 Who is he that condemneth? It is Christ that died, yea rather, that is risen again, who is even at the right hand of God, **WHO ALSO MAKETH INTERCESSION FOR US.**

Jesus never takes a vacation; He never steps aside from His duties. And no one but Jesus can act as our High Priest and Mediator or Intercessor with the Father.

In the original Greek, the word translated "intercession" is a technical term for approaching a king. Therefore, this scripture means that Christ is seeking the presence and hearing of God on behalf of others.

He is there where He ever liveth to make intercession for us, seeking the hearing of God on our behalf. When we come through Christ, we have a guaranty to get the attention of God. We cannot approach Him in any other way except through His Son.

Yet so many people try to get God to hear and answer their prayers on some other basis. This is not to say that I don't believe in good works — I do. I believe in living right. But God is not going to hear and answer your prayers on the basis of good works, although He will reward you for them.

It is puzzling to many to see faithful church workers fail to receive their healing while others, who are less committed to Christ, are healed instantly.

A pastor once told me of a man for whom he had prayed. When he arrived at the man's home, he found him partially paralyzed. The doctor had said that the man would not work another day in his life. His left arm and leg were paralyzed, and he had extreme difficulty in speaking.

The pastor thought, *Well, I'll just anoint this fellow with oil and pray for him. No doubt he's heavily sedated now, so I'll come back in a few days to find out whether he is saved. I might eventually get him healed.* So he anointed him with oil and left.

When he returned a few days later, the man's wife was in the yard, raking leaves. The pastor asked, "How is your husband getting along?"

"Oh, he's just fine," she replied. "He's working on the job. The Lord healed him."

Incredulous, the pastor drove over to where the man was working. Sure enough, he found him on top of the house, putting on a roof. The pastor sat in his car and watched as this sixty-year-old man, who the doctor had said would never work another day in his life, climbed up and down the ladder carrying shingles for the roof!

The pastor just couldn't understand how this man whose salvation he was unsure of, could receive such a marvelous healing from God, while some dedicated members of his church who had been prayed for by himself and every visiting evangelist, still weren't healed.

The pastor asked me, "Why won't God heal those who have been such fine Christian workers for so many years, yet He healed this fellow who has never even been in my church?"

Too many people think that God should heal them on the basis of good works; that He is under obligation to do something for them. However, if we could come to God through our good works, there would be no need for Jesus to function in His ministry of Intercessor. Jesus ever lives to make intercession for us, seeking God on our behalf, and we must come to God by Him. The Greek word for "intercede" means *to plead*. He ever lives to *plead* for us.

When this man approached God for his healing, it was not on his own merits that he came, but through the Name of Christ Jesus — the man just threw himself on the mercy of God. "*Let us therefore come boldly unto the throne of grace, that we may obtain mercy . . .*" (Heb. 4:16). Others, however, come pleading their own righteousness.

Sometimes when I have a healing service, I like to have the congregation sing, "Just As I Am, Without One Plea," even though I am praying for Christians.

A woman once asked me, "Brother Hagin, you know that there isn't a better Christian in this church than Momma."

I agreed with her.

She went on, "The rest of the family are all faithful Christians too. Yet I don't know of anyone in my family who has ever been healed. We always end up going to a hospital and being operated on, or just dying.

"In my husband's family it's a different story. They attend

church, but seem to serve God half-heartedly. Yet if any of them have failed to get healed, I don't know it — even the most unfaithful one in the bunch. Can you tell me why this is?"

I said, "I don't know your husband's family, but according to what God's Word teaches, could it be that they are quick to repent, forgive, and believe God?"

She exclaimed, "Yes! You are right about that. I don't think I've ever seen people who will repent as quickly as they do. They never hold a grudge against anyone. My family is always the other way around — slow to repent, slow to forgive — and it would take them forever to *believe* anything!"

She had gotten right to the heart of the problem and had diagnosed her own case. When her family saw they were wrong, they were slow to admit it.

During the Gold Rush, people panned a little gold dust in the rivers, and some found a few nuggets lying on the ground, but to get down to the real vein of gold, they had to dig for it. So it is with the Word of God. You can go along reading the Bible on the surface, and you can pick up quite a bit, but if you will stop and dig a little, it is amazing what you will find.

HEBREWS 7:25
25 Wherefore he is able also to save them to the uttermost that come unto God by him, seeing he ever liveth to make intercession for them.

I looked up the word "save" in the Greek. It is *sozo,* a word also translated "heal" and "whole" in the New Testament. Jesus used this word when He said to the woman with the issue of blood, ". . . Daughter . . . thy faith hath made thee whole . . ."* (Matt. 9:22).

"Whole" is the same word translated "save" in Hebrews 7:25. We could read Hebrews 7:25 as, "He is able also to *heal* them to the uttermost," or "to make them *whole* to the uttermost that come unto God by Him."

This explains how this man could be healed even though he might not have been in close fellowship with the Lord. Of course, God doesn't heal Christians *because* they have poor church attendance; He heals them because they come to Him the right way.

God always possesses the quality of mercy. Mercy is often lacking in mankind.

When my own brother was injured once and wasn't in fellowship with God, I thought, *Well, he is just going to have to pay for his wrongdoings.* But the Lord healed him!

Many times I have heard believers say, referring to fellow Christians, "That's good enough for them — they had it coming!"

However, even though man doesn't always show mercy, God does. He knows the whole situation, and He is faithful and merciful.

We read in James 5:14 and 15: *"Is any sick among you? let him call for the elders of the church; and let them pray over him, anointing him with oil in the name of the Lord: And the prayer of faith shall save the sick, and the Lord shall raise him up; AND IF HE HAVE COMMITTED SINS, THEY SHALL BE FORGIVEN HIM."*

It is easy for us to say, "Well, I never would do that. If I were in his place, I never would be guilty of that." But if you *were* in his situation, you might not do *as well as* he did. So instead of criticizing people, let's pray for them.

Jesus is praying for them. He ever liveth to make intercession, and He is able to heal to the uttermost those who come to God *by Him*. You can't get to the Father any other way.

Jesus is *the Way:* for being saved, for being made whole, for healing, for receiving the baptism in the Holy Spirit, for having material needs met, and for receiving answers to prayers.

We can come to the Father in the Name of Jesus.

Chapter 4
Jesus Christ, Our Shepherd

The LORD is my shepherd; I shall not want.
— Psalm 23:1

I am the good shepherd, and know my sheep. . . .
— John 10:14

In the preceding chapters we have seen Jesus as our High Priest, Advocate, Mediator, and Intercessor. He has another ministry as well: He is the Lord and Head of the Church.

David prophesied of Him in Psalm 23, *"The Lord is my shepherd; I shall not want."* And Jesus said, *"I am the good shepherd . . ."* (John 10:14).

Psalm 22 contains a prophecy of Jesus' death; Psalm 23 is a prophecy of Him as the Good Shepherd. In Psalm 24, we have a prophecy concerning the fact that Jesus is the coming King of kings and Lord of lords.

We are living right now in Psalm 23. It belongs to us. It is more than just a beautiful passage of Scripture. David is prophesying when he said, "*The Lord is my shepherd; I shall not want.*" I like to say it this way, "The Lord is my shepherd; I do *not* want."

Christ is the Caretaker, the Lover, the Bridegroom of the Body. He is the Lord and Head of the Church. He is the Firstborn from the dead.

COLOSSIANS 1:18
18 And he is the head of the body, the church: who is the beginning, the firstborn from the dead; that in all

things he might have the preeminence.

He is the Head of all principality and power. He is my risen Lord, seated at the right hand of Majesty on High.

This means that you as a Christian are an absolute overcomer. It means that poverty, want, and need are things of the past.

Philippians 4:19 says, *"But my God shall supply all your need according to his riches in glory by Christ Jesus."* Your Heavenly Father knows your needs. Jesus demonstrated that when He was on earth. He fed the multitude; He gave the disciples a great catch of fish; He turned water unto wine; He healed the sick; and He met every need of man.

That is my Lord, my Shepherd Lord. I can say, "The Lord is

my Shepherd, I do not want. I do
not want for healing. I do not
want for health. I do not want for
strength. I do not want for power.
I do not want for ability. I do not
want for money. I do not want for
anything! The Lord is my Shepherd. I do not want!"

I can say that in the face of
apparent want. I can say that in
the face of apparent defeat,
because I am walking by faith, not
sight. The Bible said we walk by
faith and not by sight (2 Cor. 5:7).
My sight may tell me it isn't so,
but if I am to please God, I am
going to have to learn to walk by
faith and to think God's thoughts
after Him.

Isaiah 55:9 says, *"For as the
heavens are higher than the earth,
so are my* [God] *ways higher than
your ways, and my thoughts than
your thoughts."*

*You can't think in the natural
and think God's thoughts.* When

you think naturally, you are thinking in the human realm. Dare to think God's thoughts! His thoughts are as high above the thoughts of men as the heavens are above the earth.

Romans 4:17 shows us God's thinking concerning Abraham: *". . . before him whom he believed, even God, who quickeneth the dead, and calleth those things which be not as though they were."* In other words, God sees things as they *are*, not as they *seem*.

If you are going to think God's thoughts, you'll see things as God sees them, not as they seem from the natural standpoint.

God told Abraham, *"Neither shall thy name any more be called Abram, but thy name shall be Abraham; for a father of many nations have I made thee"* (Gen. 17:5).

Notice God didn't say, "I AM GOING TO MAKE YOU a father

of many nations." He said, "I HAVE MADE YOU a father of many nations." He called those things which be not as though they were, and Abraham believed God.

Not only should you think like God; you also should *act* like God. You are His child, and you should partake of the Father's nature. But as long as you are thinking in the natural, your actions will be in the natural.

When God told Abraham that he would be the father of many nations, Abraham was about ninety-nine years old, and his wife Sarah, was barren! But Abraham believed God. In the natural, Abraham could not have had even one child, much less be the father of many nations. Still, he believed God.

And God brought it to pass so that Abraham's seed are as numberless as the sands of the sea and the stars of the heavens. *Believing brings it to pass in the natural realm.*

This truth is so simple we stumble over the simplicity of it. We want to make it complicated. And we do complicate it with our natural, human reasoning.

Just as we trust Christ to be our Mediator, our Intercessor, our Advocate before the Heavenly Father, we also should trust Him as our Shepherd, our Keeper, the Supplier of our needs, and the Giver of life more abundant.

The high priestly ministry of Jesus meets every need of the believer from the moment he is born again until he is ushered into the Presence of God at the end of life.

Christ has commissioned us to go and tell others of the provisions He has made for them to enter into this abundant life: knowing Christ as Savior, Mediator, Intercessor, Advocate, and Shepherd. The world cannot know if we remain silent.

Christ wants us to tell the sinner that he has been liberated; that Christ took man's sinful nature upon Himself. Christ wants us to tell the sinner that He is not holding his sins against him anymore.

Second Corinthians 5:17 and 18 says, *"Therefore if any man be in Christ, he is a new creature: old things are passed away; behold, all things are become new. And all things are of God, who . . . hath given to us the ministry of reconciliation."*

This, therefore, is the ministry that Christ has given us: the ministry of reconciliation. Verse 19 continues, *"To wit, that God was in Christ, reconciling the world unto himself, not imputing their trespasses unto them; and hath*

*committed unto us the word of rec-
onciliation."*

The word "imputing" is an
accounting term. Another translation of the above verse reads,
"He is not counting up or holding
against men their trespasses."

Some might argue, "Well, if
Christ isn't holding men's sins
against them, they will automat-
ically be saved."

No, the reason men must be
saved is because we are all born
in sin and must be born again in
Christ. Christ is not interested in
holding man's sins against him.
Christ is interested in drawing
man to Himself.

When D. L. Moody began
preaching, every one of his sermons was on the judgment of
God. He said, "I would preach
every day on the text that God is
angry with the sinner. That kind
of preaching got a few people
saved."

Once when Moody was visiting England, he casually told a nineteen-year-old boy, "If you ever come to America, come preach for me." Moody later admitted he had extended the invitation more out of courtesy than sincerity. Two years later, Moody answered a knock on his front door only to find this young preacher ready to take him up on his invitation.

Of course, there was nothing to do but offer his pulpit to the young man for a week of services. Sunday night, the opening night of the revival, the boy preached from John 3:16. On Monday, Mr. Moody had to leave town for previously scheduled speaking engagements, so he told his wife and church leaders that the young man's revival services could be held in the church basement during his absence. Moody was certain that not many people would turn out to hear this novice preacher.

Moody returned home from his preaching tour after the Thursday night service. Fearing the worst, he asked his wife how the services were going. To his surprise she replied, "Oh, last night we had to move into the main auditorium, and tonight it was packed and overflowing with people."

Shocked that the young preacher was drawing larger crowds than he was, Moody asked, "Well, what in the world is he preaching on?"

Mrs. Moody answered, "He's preaching on the same thing every night — John 3:16."

Moody went on to say that this experience changed his ministry. He never again preached on the judgment of God; He preached on the love of God. He said, "And where I had gotten one saved before, I am getting one hundred saved now."

Christ, *"hath committed unto us the word of reconciliation."* He wants us to go and tell the lost that He is *"not imputing their trespasses unto them."*

The Amplified Bible translation of Second Corinthians 5:19 reads, "It was God [personally present] in Christ, reconciling and restoring the world to favor with Himself, not counting up and holding against [men] their trespasses [but cancelling them], and committing to us the message of reconciliation (of the restoration to favor)."

The sinner does not need to think that God is mad at him or that God is against him. *The sin that sends a man to hell is not an act or deed, such as lying, stealing, or cheating; it is rejecting the Lord Jesus Christ!*

John 16:7-9 says, *"Nevertheless I tell you the truth; It is expedient for you that I go away: for if I go not away, the Comforter will not come unto you; but if I depart, I will send him unto you. And when he is come, he will reprove the world of sin, and of righteousness, and of judgment: Of sin, because they believe not on me."*

Every man has a right to know of Christ's saving grace.

Every man has a right to know that Christ will meet all his needs — that Christ will be his High Priest, Advocate, Mediator, Intercessor, and Shepherd.

A Sinner's Prayer To Receive Jesus as Savior

Dear Heavenly Father,

I come to You in the Name of Jesus.

Your Word says, "*. . . him that
cometh to me I will in no wise cast
out*"
(John 6:37),

So I know You won't cast me out,
but You take me in,

And I thank You for it.

You said in Your Word, "*Whosoever
shall call upon the name of the
Lord shall be saved*"
(Rom. 10:13).

I am calling on Your name,

So I know You have saved me now.

You also said, "*. . . if thou shalt
confess with thy mouth the Lord
Jesus, and shalt believe in thine
heart that God hath raised him
from the dead, thou shalt be*

*saved. For with the heart man
believeth unto righteousness; and
with the mouth confession is
made unto salvation"*
(Rom. 10:9,10).

I believe in my heart that Jesus
Christ is the Son of God.

I believe that He was raised from
the dead for my justification.

And I confess Him now as my Lord,

Because Your Word says, "*. . .with
the heart man believeth unto
righteousness. . .*" and I do believe
with my heart,

I have now become the righteousness of God in Christ
(2 Cor. 5:21),

And I am saved!

Thank You, Lord!

Signed _____

Date _____

About the Author

Kenneth E. Hagin ministered for almost 70 years after God miraculously healed him of a deformed heart and an incurable blood disease at the age of 17. Even though Rev. Hagin went home to be with the Lord in 2003, the ministry he founded continues to bless multitudes around the globe. Kenneth Hagin Ministries' radio program, *Rhema for Today*, is heard on more than 150 stations nationwide and on the Internet worldwide. Other outreaches include *The Word of Faith*, a free monthly magazine; crusades conducted throughout the nation; RHEMA Correspondence Bible School; RHEMA Bible Training Center; RHEMA Alumni Association; RHEMA Ministerial Association International; RHEMA Supportive Ministries Association; and a prison outreach.

Word of Faith

The *Word of Faith* is a full-color magazine
with faith-building teaching articles by
Rev. Kenneth E. Hagin and
Rev. Kenneth Hagin Jr.

The *Word of Faith* also includes encouraging
true-life stories of Christians overcoming
circumstances through God's Word, and
information on the various outreaches of
Kenneth Hagin Ministries
and RHEMA Bible Church.
To receive a free subscription to
The Word of Faith, call:

1-888-28-FAITH—Offer #P014
(1-888-283-2484)
www.rhema.org/wof